Love And Hate

Love And Hate

First Edition

No. _____

Book & Cover Design
Minerva Designs

Back Cover Photograph
Clarence Johns

for   *Jim Henson*
         Carol
         Richard Mathews
         Laurel
         Billy Collins
         Heidi
         Gianfranco Spavieri
         Silva
         Joseph Ross
         Beatrix
         Mike Garn
         Elena
         Frederick Park
         Cristina

Love And Hate

© 2005 by Lawrence Johns

All Rights Reserved

No part of this publication may be reproduced or transmitted in any form or by any means, electronic or mechanical, including photocopy, fax, email or recording, or any information storage and retrieval system, including computers, servers, the internet or world wide web, without permission in writing from the publisher.

Library Of Congress
Control Number: 2004094136

ISBN: 1929096038

Conscious Publishing
POB 80262
Portland, Oregon 97280

www.consciouspublishing.com

Lawrence Johns

Love And Hate

CONSCIOUS

Also by Lawrence Johns

Sensazioni

Love And Hate

Looking For The Perfect Rock

Owsley's purple dome rushes hot

Somewhere chill near Bonny Doon

Where the magnetic hum of Darby's Ridge

Brings the vortex history of earth

Streaming to a tripper's eyes

And the search for the perfect rock

Starts with the one in your hand

Sammy examines by lemon morning light

Drawn to the clear profiles of horned Alexander

And laughing Einstein in the lichen

They carry the deeper memory

Of heavymetal birth in a star's demise

And the betrayal of time by sweet running distance

He sees volcanoes spew uncertainty

And continents lose their roots

But right where it starts to make sense

With the flash of human Will

A legion of purple paisley acid worms

Invades the frame of reference

Exploding into R Crumb's amazons

All monster thighs butts

Hairy legs and stormtrooper boots

So with a thick question mark

Hanging in a bubble of panic

Sammy finds himself running the trail

Looking for new stories

He's taking a breather under black oak

When the notion arrives to spread them out

Give them some air let's take a look

Ten fifteen eighteen faces

Arranged in alluring horseshoe

Like the girls at Mustang Ranch

Surely the perfect rock is here

The World is poised to reveal itself today

A bluejay swoops down

A hundred a thousand bluejays

Connecting each tree to a lucky synapse

High in the billowing clouds

He sees the smoky trains of Consciousness

Slow and stop in a silent whistle of attention

Every motion frozen by the intuition

That says Being can't really move at all

But he feels the intense desire of each rock to go home

So shouting out constellations like stations

He starts throwing his collection

Up through the Douglas firs

Across the accumulator banks of dark matter

And back to the hydrogen dance of first Becoming

He's saying his long goodbye to the Goethe granite

When the first lava shudder shakes his spine

Looking closer it's late afternoon

It's time to find the Ford van

Time to crank the starter

Finger his black moustache

Then ease downhill to the Full Rack Saloon

And his usual double shot of Wild Turkey

That signals the end of the trip

He's coaxing the heater

Cajoling bald tires

Thinking Billy turns cartoons into poems

Like Warhol paints Marilyns

And acid makes music of a mountain road

Time to hit the gravel parking lot

Stumble into the Full Rack

And introduce his comedown to the crowd

At the mahogany bar he's pulling out a jackson

When the sound of one rock hitting the floor

Stops the roaring biker buzz

Every eye is upon him as he picks up

And drops it in his glass

He's thirsty Sammy explains

As the chunk of quartz rattles and drains the bourbon

Spent the day up on Darby's Ridge

Looking for a perfect mind

But now nobody cares

So he orders another drink

And warms to the idea that when you really find something

It always finds you first

Flick The On Switch

Feather's fearless heart comes from two things

Run to market right after her first period

The pink contraception wheel shattering windows

In West Virginian houses of American Straight

And her raccoon couplings with local boys

Transformed into science fiction by a magic sugar cube

She's trying to switch the foster parents

Who bought her from a photo album

For the liberal ladies at Wheeling Planned Parenthood

Tracking her tragedy with lemon sugar cookies

At fifteen she's trying to fall in love with Love

Feeling the mythic pulse of pleasure in every stroke

She's busted for servicing her English teacher

Between classes in the second floor broom closet

The vacuum cleaner hose banging on linoleum

Is her last memory of Madison High

As her current set of fosters call the parish priest

About an exorcism for this pixie girl

Who's always scratching in church

The collar's drinking Earl Grey in the living room

When she slides down the drainpipe

Clutching her autoharp and directions to the Haight

The tin cans look rustier in the ditches

The crows blacker in their babble

As she runs under a hot rockabilly sun

Nothing can break her Celtic heart

Nothing can block this mystic unfolding

She makes love to every man boy who asks polite

And an old lady in Boulder who paints her portrait

On hoarded French cream canvas

Her love is infinite and becomes fair exchange

For food clothes and shelter along the American highway

Truckers thinking they have a runaway to rape

Are transformed into penitent dads after a hug

Salesmen hoping to cloud a life of lies

With casual perversions find their minds blown

By the simple lubrication of a kiss

Hippies instinctively treat her as their queen

Presenting keys to the new underground railroad

Smoking runaway slaves to San Francisco

Standing in the bathroom of a Moab motel

She confirms her cosmic necessity

Applauds her purple eye and filling figure

Half Liz Taylor half Indian

Dressed in fresh buckskin

Radiant in bald eagle feathers

Dangling beads and tiny mirrors

So tuned to Love

That every city erects to greet her

The word is out in the Berkeley Hills

And everyone is so kind she postpones

Her entry into the Haight

Until everybody else gets there first

Flyers are posted along Telegraph Avenue

The Goddess of Love is here

Receiving at 2793 Benvenue

And after two surreal months

In the city named for the English idealist

Feather discovers she can come at will

Her lovers are erotic images of the World

Momentarily freed from the machineries of Hate

Embracing her bluegrass tunes

Kneeling before her temple of hair and heat

Giving what they came to take

Watching their every chain break

She whispers you are free

You are free Love is free you are free

Love is forever you are forever Love is free

You are free you are Me you are free

Love is forever We are forever Love is free

You are free Love is free you are free

And now it's time

To flick the on switch

Running From Reseda

He can't hear what his father's saying

He's making a tunafish sandwich at the counter

When a bookkeeper's belt catches him on the back

And his youth falls through the kitchen floor

It's the long hair it's always the long hair

But this time Hardy's cramming skivvies

Into a green army duffel

Feeling superior to this exploding failure

He leaves his mother balancing gin tonics

On the LA Times crossword puzzle

Carefully closing the rickety patio door

In final submission to childhood conditioning

He sprints through her dead cactus garden

And down the hill to Reseda High

Seven Barbie cheerleaders tumble and grin

As he takes a memorial lap around the track

Remembering the league cross-country finals

He won as a sophomore with a monster sprint

Looking for something Wilde

To relieve nostalgia and buck his courage

Hardy vows never to talk to his father

Or sleep in his own bed again

He gets lucky at the Roscoe onramp

An insurance guy driving a Chevy

Going all the way to Chowchilla

The midnight truckstop shimmers in blue neon solitude

As Hardy sees a brunette in the window

After two coffees and a question on a napkin

He's waiting coyote at the back door

When her shift ends at 3

After two paces she has his sun sign

Says they'll meet a dragon tonight

Pouring supermarket Tom Collins

Meryl takes him as her astrological disciple

Passing on the same passion and scientific precision

That ruined her life

She introduces him to twelve types of orgasm

Corresponding to the Sumerian zodiac

And asks him to repair the ductape

Holding her Airstream trailer together

He's quickly addicted to her scent

Sliding gratefully on arcana sheets

Carefully forgetting the details

To protect a new sense of manly pride

And then there's nothing more to learn

So he leaves Meryl sleeping before dawn

Running three miles of freeway with his duffel

Feeling the sun rise out of his right ear

At a Texaco station he catches a ride

With a confidence man talking to himself

Hey Conrad I've seen this face before

In the Times or Chess Life

Check it out Conrad we got a junior master in the back seat

So for a double cheeseburger Hardy hips him

To some Russian novelties in the Petroff Defense

Moving the button magnets in the traveling set

Reminds him of her ephemeris

And the dull rivets of her aluminum cocoon

Showing the salesman a tricky rook and pawn ending

Hardy switches to his new voice

I see you're Gemini with Scorpio rising

You think everything's a game

And people fearful greedy pieces

Your simplicity is your profundity

But if you don't get into communications

Your life will slowly dissolve into poverty

His comments define the long drive

As they silently watch dust devils

Hide power lines in California valley heat

And when they hit San Jose

Conrad gives him $40 and an address in Oakland

Where he can stay for a few days

The Vanity Of Man

Chatting with the ghost of La Rochefoucauld

Erin extends the vanity of Man to cover

The idea of the Idea

Adjusting the rhinestone net on her auburn hair

She spins and peeks in the hall mirror

Timing her reflections for the nameless screenwriters

Begging to put words in her mouth

She pauses to admire the last magentas

Splayed across the granite thighs of Coit Tower

Checks her measuring devices

A final acrylic coat on her nails

A toss of a peacock shawl

And down to the parking garage

Reaching under the red vinyl seat of her Mustang

For the coke baggie and a fat white snake

Quicksnorted on the console

Through a hundred dollar bill

Looking at the grim concrete wall in the rearview mirror

She concedes the point to Schopenhauer

Isn't the Will to Life the quintessence of vanity?

Isn't stylish retreat into Art

The only way to deal with heinous reality?

She curses her way through North Beach stripper traffic

Honking for punctuation

Pointing her red gelding towards Pacific Heights

And the party at the Millford House

Flocks of white jackets and oriental faces

Jockey for the keys

As Erin attacks San Francisco's liberal elite

Preening like seals in the ballroom

She elbows her way through buckskin g-strings

Translucent saris psychedelic bell-bottoms

Wincing at the champagne gush

On Crowley Trotsky Timothy Leary

Without hard purpose she'd be lost here

Carried to some irretrievably mad beach

Buffeted by the cynical winds of fashion

And reclaimed by pessimism

She takes the gilded elevator to the master bedroom

Arranges the lights so they converge

On the bay window reflector

A stick of sandalwood incense

Pacing

She awaits her first client

Smoking a Sherman's cigarette

Selling her aristocratic profile

To the omnipresent brokers of fame

He's Derec with a c

Joking cautiously about the $50 fee

They all do

Then sweating like a truant surfer

Before the hidden contractions of the Polaroid

She knows the rhythms of the vain

She calms him down with routine questions

About his childhood and baseball

Then right to it

Derec I'm going to create the conditions

Where you can see your aura

The biomagnetic force that's your inner Being

You'll feel a slight cooling

Or a slight warming

And I'll always be in control

Are you ready?

Turn to the window

And think of your greatest pleasure

Think of your Power

Pausing

Allowing the man to lock it in

They're all the same

Yes I can see something forming

Yes this is amazing

The purple in the second corona

Indicates great psychic potential

If you keep to the spiritual path

You'll be successful in whatever you choose to do

Derec mentions his grandmother

In San Antonio

Standing tense as she takes the calipers out

To measure his vortex of vanity

This is rare

You have a white flame piercing the purple

Which means advanced sexual prowess

If you use it wisely

You can lift the seven veils of Aphrodite

Rouse the sacred snake of kundalini

Pointing

Your pictures are ready

See the auras here

And there

She closes him with a smile

Derec drops a big bill

In her wicker fishing basket

They all do

He's lingering at the door

It's a scam isn't it?

All this hippie Love stuff is a con

For a second she thinks he might be a cop

But Manny

Philip K

Paul Reggie and Dick are hot

Their bodies clouding and condensing the mystic

Until the windows cry

Her personal record is nineteen

But today she burns out at eleven

Marveling once again at the hermetic mystery

In a normal mix of seekers and jerks

The camera captures two or three real auras

Isn't this the biggest joke?

That illusion trips up reality?

That the Will to Life is the Lie

Making Truth of every stubborn instant?

She knows she'll be seeing dark shadows hanging

From every zipper in town for days

And the frost of deep emotional distaste

In every breath she takes

She guns the car out to Land's End

Aiming the Esplanade

Angry south to Pacifica

And a quick trade of her dirty money

For pure Colombian snow

And a white night rapping politics with her friends

Back on Stanyan

What's the best way to bring Revolution to the streets?

What's with the New Left coalitions?

Around 4 Bobby Seale shows up in his bomber jacket

And shotgun bodyguards

How do we get the Jewish money honey?

You got any contacts in New York?

Who's your man honey who's your main man?

With a habit like that you need a big dog

A real big dog

Dawn finds her driving asleep

With her eyes wired open

Pointing her Mustang home

With the small muscles in her wrists

Agreeing with Empedocles

Love and Hate are the motors of Being

Despite brilliant intent

In the winedark sea of human experience

All we can do is steer

Breakfast At Denny's

First as pure literary conceit

Then as existential duty

The thought of icing Jackson is born

In the desire to match intense sensation

With a suitably dramatic act

Frank finally hunts Jackson down

At the Highlander student café

With a thriftstore salmon knife

Hidden in the lining of his jacket

After three weeks of accidental evasion

Jackson's definitely here

Dragging fries through a gymkhana of catsup

His regimental Brook Brothers tie

Thrown casual over his left shoulder

Here's the Dick Tracy unshaven jaw

The Atlanta cowlick and polio limp

He's the name Penny called when she cameflood

And Frank's here to kill him quick

For the jealousy he never knew

And the novel he'll never finish

In this film his only thought is contrast

Where madness is measured against madness

And first Love is the famous blind director

When she kicks him out he parks on the corner

Where he can watch both doors

Attacking time by writing haiku on the dash

And burning maxims in her burmuda

With cheap Arco gas

Painting the sidewalk brown

Her snails whining Dali

Dali

He sees violence and perfect memory

As natural consequences of existential philosophy

Transcended by loss into Pop Art

Would you like some fries?

It threw him off just enough

Are you up for a little stud tonight?

I've got seven hundred cash in my pocket

Been looking for a game

So Frank ditches the knife behind magnolia

And follows Jackson to the parking lot

Relieved to exit another bad French film

He's following the Jaguar XK-140

By transmission howl and rattle

Down University Avenue through Riverside

To an old gray Victorian in the wash

He parks his van beside a sunken porch

Suffocated by fallen willows

Blown up the steps and in

By the curious winds of competition

Little seven-card stud head to head nothing wild table stakes

Ten minute break every two hours food's in the fridge

Have a shot of this

Jackson pours Frank three fingers of Jack Daniels'

Down the road you'll appreciate this Shark

Playing cards is far better than hard time

Jackson laughs

Nobody's worth it

And poker plays to your dreams it's your deal

A naked hundred-watt bulb hangs over the table

On a tangled beige cord

A wind kicks up sending sand through broken panes

As Frank shuffles the plastic KEM cards

Thinking well met

Maybe this is the worthy opponent Nietzsche was seeking

A singular focus for the Hate seething inside

Jackson's losing heavily on blind raises and baby trips

Frank's over two hundred to the good

Without ever touching his back pocket

Cognizant of the trap but too cruising to care

The subtle blend of cheap whiskey

Wind and classical conversation goes to his head

You know Shark we're missing the boat down here

All the action's up in the Haight

The World's being born anew

Might get interesting

During drunken stretches when Jackson catches cards

He chips away at Frank's stack

But as the angry hiss of gila monsters waking

Signals another hot and smoggy Riverside dawn

Frank pockets the seven for scientific play

And accepts Jackson's check for three more

Thinking only friendships formed over stud

Are strong enough to withstand the vagaries of time

Losing Penny was the only way to find an adversary

Strong enough to inspire new identities

It's already over eighty in the Mover's Service van

As Frank enters the dreamless sleep of winners

Waking in a cold sweat around nine-thirty

Immediately confirmed by the missing Jag

It's a grainy drive through fresh-clipped palms

To the tall glass doors of Great Western Savings

When Jackson tools into the lot belching oil

Hey Shark the check's rubber let's have breakfast at Denny's

They're sitting in the baby blue vinyl booth

Talking of synchronicity

Two orders of chicken-fried steak and eggs for me

And whatever my friend wants says Jackson

Checking his Rolex

And making for the restroom

Frank's wrestling with pancake options

When the waitress returns with coffee

Is it Penny?

He's far too tired to tell

Same oval face big breasts

A bolt in recent memory explodes

And he remembers how they timed the waterbed

Like telepathic dolphins

Coming together perfectly every ninth wave

Then suspicious

Frank runs out to the lot

His van is gone

Thanks for the trade Shark

Says a note under the wiper

Don't try to pass the cash

I have to be Frisco tonight stay in touch

Buddha's Body

Rikki's raised diamondbacks since she was eight

Keeping them slow with small white mice

Now she sells the venom mail order

To pay for her Harley

Popping wheelies in the Palos Verdes High parking lot

To rankle the jocks and Straights

Her only steady is a set of Wilson Staffs

Slung over her shoulder Duke of Windsor style

She's busted for selling grass to an undercover cop

Posing as a Golf Magazine reporter

It's the same as feeding pinkeyes to my rattlers

It makes them happy and conversational

What's wrong with that?

Her inventor father sneaks another scotch

Her mom's silence says it all

The deputy DA with a military buzzcut

Gives her the choice of two to twenty

For felony narcotics

Or a rare chance with the Army Rangers

Starting tomorrow in Monterey

Nobody can get you out of this one kid

We want Palos Verdes clean

Every judge in this county has a runaway daughter

That started with a joint in school you're cooked

Better sign on take your chances in Nam

And do what no other girl has done

She looks him coy in the eye

Pulls him closer with his stained tie

And headbutts his nose

Given her Mensa intelligence

She easily outscores the eighty-nine others

Testing to become CIA code and language experts

So on her eighteenth birthday she's shipped to Saigon

To translate the tortured confessions of NLF officers

Into American primetime English

The dependence of her superiors on sleep deprivation

Torture and sexual humiliation

Changes her idea of information forever

She spends her downtime devising an unbreakable code

So she can talk to herself

To the hundreds of Xs left on her arm by snakebites

She adds Os with a tattoo needle

And soon the other Rangers know

She gets first crack at every new horse

The minute it hits the barracks

The heroin helps her concentration

And hides the pain of daddy's daughter

Grown to look like a boy

After three months in Nam she's a junkie

With a heavy habit and the nodder's trick

Of playing every end against the middle

The more outrageous she acts

The more undercover they think she is

Navy thinks she's Army the Marines think she's Navy

And the CIA thinks she's working a Presidential folder

She comes and goes as she pleases

So the brass ignores it when she hits the field

To debrief a Viet Cong colonel

Selling dates of an upcoming offensive for $2 million

And a day at Disneyland for his family

When she goes AWOL the General Staff stiffens

Calls it MIA and sends the Rangers in

To take care of their own

She's working towards the border

Through booby-trapped tunnels following a rumor

Of an old Buddhist monk

Carving cosmic language in a needle tree

She finds him a mile from Cambodia sixty feet up

She climbs the platform

Rolls up her sleeves and sees a heart blast off

Behind his expressionlessness

I have never met a mind like yours

I have been working on Buddha's body for twenty-two years

Trying to write the sacred code in a living thing

Will you stay to help me?

Rikki takes the rope down

Comes back in an hour

With three small barbequed pythons

And some boiled greens

You are a new kind of woman

What is your belief?

I love the future of Man

The old Buddhist understands more in Rikki's reply

Than she thinks

And while they carve the meaning of Buddha's body

Into the reddish-brown bark

They come to shared conclusions

They see the World as a lost monkey

In a multidimensional jungle of dark energies

They feel the steady pull of expanding Consciousness

And the wrenching tragedy of personal affection

They travel to new locations in the multiverse

Riding white cones of rippling photons

And while the old man soars his hand wanders

Doubt has raised the ancient defenses

He gets nasty when she goes into the green for her fix

Sentimental when she brings him hot rice

One afternoon after lunch he's on the big branch

Starting a promising new paragraph

When Love attacks and he falls

No spot of ochre hitting no ground

Once the obligatory hooting and clowning are over

The monks pass on the master's final request

Can you complete Buddha's body?

Yes

Can you stay?

No

Rikki takes a final look up the needle tree

And heads back to the tunnels

Determined to get lost like Chet Baker

The One-Club Match

She edges into the village of Bu Prang

When she needs rice and butane

And collapses in the arms of kids

Who keep her alive on ratmeat and wellwater

Until she goes cold turkey in a cave

Preferring any hallucination to her memories

She wanders the rice patties seeking solace

And finds small pieces of natural rubber

That she makes into golf balls

And scores with her Ranger knife

Thinking of the fight between Old Tom Morris

And Alan Robertson

Will the featherie endure

Or will the guttie dominate because it's cheap

And flies better when wet?

She's fifteen

Short blonde hair square jaw

Big hitter

Leading local qualifying for the U.S. Women's Open

By six shots

Coming into the last hole at Long Beach Municipal

Her drive on the par five splits the middle

But she can't find the ball

She starts to tornado around the missing white center

And walks off the course

Disqualified and suddenly qualified for far worse

She always does it right and it always goes wrong

Her life becomes recovering from shock

And surviving her suffering

Here she persists by teaching golf to kids

The proper grip the proper turn then let it rip

With clubs made of downed fighter parts

And balls that hang in the wind

The grateful village chief offers his hut

The only one with a working toilet

So Rikki sleeps

And sleeps some more

Regaining her strength

Until she hears a tinker

Hawking titanium scrap

From American attack choppers

She makes up three starter sets

She's playing with her students in the mud

When she sees the ghost of the old monk

Putting out at the 3rd

She's got a better idea

OK let's keep it simple kids

Let's respect the duality of past and present

Let's respect our many selves

If Rikki At Fifteen wins she goes back to her outfit

If Rikki At Eighteen wins she goes to San Francisco

And stops the War

She twirls the four-iron in her hand

Formally nodding once left once right

So we're agreed

It's a one-club match for everything

It's your honor

Rikki At Fifteen hits a good drive

Long and straight with the trailing wind

Golf shot says Rikki At Eighteen

But it never came down

The Word After Beastly

At the City Lights bookstore

Sammy reads a poem by Gary Snyder

About blooming rhododendrons in Oregon

And decides to confront this subtle mind

He sells his collection of Swift essays to Ferlinghetti

Takes a night flight to Tokyo

A crowded train and he's decompressing Kyoto

Soaking in hot perfumed baths

His long black hair in samurai knots

The morning chilly and overcast

As Sammy sets out north

Past the hungry intelligence of Zen rock gardens

And the slow breathing of ancient moss

A mile upstream he's got the house

Met on dragon tiles by Gary's wife

Led to a waiting room of blonde bamboo

Then a dark cherry studio

The Beat poet who gave hippies their name

The original Dharma Bum

Declines to turn around

Sammy says I've come a long way for this

I'm working go away

What's the word after beastly?

It wasn't the question he came to ask

It was an ejaculation

Provoked by Snyder's fingers

Marching like army ants through the Oxford Dictionary

To search and store the word of the day

Thinking reverence for authority

Is the Beats' comic flaw

Sammy starts to make the sound of one hand clapping

With his foot

When a perfumed Aikido move

Has him splashing in the carp pool

Laughing at himself

A Small Jewel

Toby's cutting across People's Park

A good thirty minutes

Ahead of his appointment with Feather

Pausing like Dr Watson to strike a match

And smoke a joint

Beneath his gray bowler hat

He imagines her carried by devotees

On a small jewel couch above the World

Smiling with all-embracing wisdom

At every strange and struggling human desire

He checks his gold pocket watch

Still thirty minutes to go

So he takes another toke

Everything above his waist

Drifting in Cleveland fantasy

And everything below

Shaking like a wet Frisbee dog

The Guitar Man

Hardy's sitting full lotus on the sidewalk

In front of the Straight Theater

His long brown beard and hair

Spilling over a cream Nehru jacket

When a chubby redhead in a thin dress says

Hi my name's Pickles

Want some free Mr Natural from Owsley?

Enchanted by her nipples pointing East West

Through crimson cheesecloth

Hardy eats two blotter cartoons

And jumps a new point of view

Seventy feet above Haight Street

Watching animals morph the clouds

And hippies george and jam the sidewalks

Until his catbird seat gets crowded

And he's cruising Golden Gate Park

Looking for a spot in the Crystal Palace Solarium

To meditate in peace

But the cranking of a rock guitar

Lures him back into the open

The Guitar Man's playing delta blues

Country with a fine jazz top

Some Charlie Christian swing chords

His horny fingers running over the frets

Like baby crabs on a blister beach

Hardy sits loaded in the elephant grass

Thinking this guy's good

Maybe better than Jerry Garcia

He can do it all

Mr Natural's starting to crackle

Hardy's vaguely getting to his feet

When he's hit by a psychic blast

And finds himself trailing seven harpies

To Charlie Manson's beige Travelall

He takes the shotgun seat

Absently pulling on his beard

As Charlie crosses the Bay Bridge three times

Waiting an hour behind a dumpster in Emeryville

Before handing out U-Nos to the crew

Hardy whistles softly the Beatle songbook

As Charlie drives the gravel pentagram

Protecting his ranch in the San Raphael hills

Thinking the man's magnetic

Maybe I can be his lyricist

On Tuesdays they slaughter the baby lambs

On Fridays it's the baby pigs

For guests it's foraging cans of corn and yams

After Charlie's harem is through with the kitchen

Hardy's spinning philosophical essays

With the cramped elegance of De Sade

Working on songs that mimic John and Paul

When he overhears Squeaky at the pool

Flapping her floaties

Charlie says it's been two months

The boy's fat enough

Hardy's over the edge running down the jackstraw slope

Leaping low retaining walls and poison oak

Looking for somebody new to serve

Burrs

Drying a Safeway bag of peyote buds

In the Electric Avenue duplex

Frank's out on the street

Tossing tennis balls to Heraclitus

When Canned Heat rolls in

Air guitars on the white couch

Chopstick fills on the white radiator

The sticky buds washed down with Rainier Ale

And windowpane acid

Somebody suggests Mount Baldy

Heraclitus is first in the white van

Claiming the center of the Sufi carpet

Blues from Muddy Waters and Son House

Droning from black plastic speakers

When a radiator hose blows a mile shy of the Euclid exit

The band hesitates on the freeway shoulder

Then Bob Hite grabs his Fender case

A sea lion sliding down the embankment

Headed for nowhere fast

Three highway patrol cruisers stop

Red and blue erupt from black and white

As Frank and the band boogie Bob's tracks

Down a concrete stormdrain

And through a twisted hurricane fence

Fear and fantasy melting in peyote vomit

Where's Heraclitus?

Coming over a sagebrush ridge

Frank hears snapping whines

And sees his dog writhing in the sand

Tearing out chunks of bloody hide

To get the burrs

Frank starts with firm commands

But only a hammerlock works

So with his heart opening a sad secret door

Frank starts pulling them out

One by one

The setting sun washes the foothills in Hollywood pastels

As a police chopper finds them with a light cannon

Stand up with your arms in the air

And walk slowly back to your vehicle

Frank continues to count

Walk slowly back to your vehicle or we open fire

At 78 Frank's hands cramp

At 215 the chopper's gone

His fingers are aliens

Screaming in mouthless alien pain

At 302 Frank loses cause and effect

Burrs are plucking bloody fingers from the fur

At 441 he flashes on the Augustine monks

And their bitter hatred of angels

Extracted one by one

From the heads of pins

As Heraclitus lies exhausted in his arms

And the Don Juan hawk

Soars on distant Mexican updrafts

Frank affirms his Hate

And starts counting the cops of California

The Material Agent

He's the son of the son of Owen Glendover

And his Welsh blood gives him the right

To ride over dreams as if they were distinctions of Will

He refuses to prefer the continuity of waking life

To what occurs to his mind while he sleeps

Even when his Celtic pride strikes genius

And gives the glint of autonomy to his actions

Experience remains more a matter of taste than memory

Was he recruited as an AFS student in Leningrad?

Trained in the intricate loyalties of the Soviet Man

And given mystic vision into the true nature of Material?

Was this a personal fantasy running deep in the blood

Or a collective spirit ruling his decisions from the blue?

Everything he does is jacketed by intellect and contradiction

Until he misses a haircut with Tony at the Mission Inn

And the Cold War stops

As red curls cover the tips of his ears

He asks himself one last question

And lets it all go

His handlers in Moscow curse

Send the local gorillas to reel him in

But they don't have a chance

Because now he feels his sensual destiny

SDS and other leftist student groups are jokes

Nobody can be a hippie like me

I am Shakespeare's every character

I am Emerson's every personality

I will inherit the earth

I am the Material Agent

I will eliminate the metaphysical

Starting with the strongest Eastern masters

He picks up a passport from a safehouse in Fremont

Next morning he's on a flight to Hong Kong

Feeling flip like Mercutio

Poxing both their houses

I'm going to take out a few gurus

He comments to the hostess

As she pours his Canada Dry ginger ale

Man

Man must be overcome

After two weeks resting at the YMCA

He's huddled in a sandblasted delivery van

With a rubber mask and cheap plastic shoes

Working out his opening moves

Against the Chan Buddhist Master

Who named the winds of Consciousness

In this film he's accepted at the back door

Of the Ma Shan Monastery

Asked to clean the chicken coops

And crease the six thousand handkerchiefs

That lie on every wooden surface

He's a background fixture at morning lectures

On the prajnaparamita sutra

Until one Saturday over gruel

When he fires from the hip

Not only is there no dust on the mirror

Not only is there no one to know it

Not only is there no enlightenment

But no one has ever been Conscious!

Red flames leap from Master Yen's eyes

As Frank escapes laughing

And works his way to Tibet

Where he varies the idea at the Portola Palace

In the heartbeat of the 500 Year-Old Man

Giant conches salute another clear win

So he carries on to India

Exposing the magic tricks of Sai Baba

Where mysterious white ash and petals in the palm

Gets the guru a Patek-Philippe or Vacheron

The son of the son of Owen Glendover

Finds he can best champion material life

By defeating the masters of metaphysical deception

Yet the more he stays in the East

Where individuation has always been suspect

The more he understands Canterbury and Rome

And his hatred for Christian faith grows

Even if he could return to the mountains with Zarathustra

And erase the fictions of Good and Evil

The moralisms of Church and State would still inform

The systematic savagery of Will To Power

And the lust for personal immortality

Chasing white pigs on a Goan blacksand beach

He sees the Indian Ocean fill his footprints

And he knows it's time to come in from the cold

A haircut at the New Delhi Intercontinental

Debriefed in Tony's heavily accented Russian

The Vietnam War's entering a crucial new phase

Your new assignment is Berkeley

Organizing the student anti-war movement

And coordinating New Left coalitions

Your ticket for San Francisco

Is under the towel

Touching down at LAX

Frank tells the cabbie Gardena

The Monterey Club

And forty minutes later he's riding the steep face of a rush

At 10-20 draw poker

Back

Back on the brushed green felt of the Wild West

First Tuesday

Erin makes First Tuesday just in time

Circling the Mime Troupe skit on Delmar

Striding briskly up familiar stairs

She rings the silver Navaho bells

Then nine luminous steps to the stool

Parker mixing walnut oil in a small jar

Trying to hide his excitement as she disrobes

Normally he's a motormouth

Hip to the slang every Black hustler needs

But on First Tuesdays he's an artist

Locked into silence by his love of the White Goddess

A mute stableboy with sable brushes and crazy notions

Holding invisible reins to impossible horses

Erin takes her pose

And drifts into thought

This is the way it should be

When the Revolution has uprooted the false and base

This is the true object of our struggle

To be adored like we were once adored

Four hundred thousand years of Her

Gives meaning to Life

We have our rituals

Our moon

Our silent and scintillating understandings

We take lovers to honor the four winds

We take kings to kill them in January

We are the great transcendence

We are the great immanence

Our daughters are the founders of cities

We are kind and relentless

We are knowing and soothing

We are the only Revolution that matters

We will destroy patriarchy

From inside our vaginas and wombs

We will turn Straight America inside out

We will make Women's Liberation our arms and legs

We will make the barter market our torso

And trade up until men become what they are

Pleasant diversions or necessary drones

And all this we will do in the name of men

For without the Goddess they will destroy the World

With their egregious lies and nuclear secrets

The hippies on the street with their snaky hair

Will be our ministers and our Dionysus

We will be in the grass and trees

And we will be in the streams and oceans

We will be in every passing cloud

And every new thunderbolt

We will rule the world from the Haight

And we will save the World from men

From its Moslems and Evangelicals

From its Puritans and Jesuits

From its troubled tribes of Jews

And all authoritarian systems

Derived from a weak and brutal Father

We will abolish the laws enacted to sanctify insanity

My sisters we lived so well without police

My sisters we lived so well without property

My sisters we lived so well without banks

And now we are policed assets

Bought at public auction

And financed by banks with the highest rates

My sisters this war in Vietnam is terrible

But war against the Goddess is worse

In truth we are all warriors for Athena

But we have been sold into slavery

By our own ignorance and fears

We have become bricabrac in plastic houses

Dressed to grace an evening on the town

Or impress some prospective client

My sisters we have all betrayed the Goddess

And we deserve our current condition

Men have constructed a World based on mathematics

Spatial orientation and technological applications

And we have fallen into their traps

Content to take them prisoner

And hold their children hostage

My sisters we have been tricked by their laws

We do not need prisoners or hostages

We do not need equal rights

We do not need equal wages

These are knots in their bloody noose

We need only to be adored

And the Goddess needs to be adored through us

That is how it is and must be

My sisters say no to the mean slavers of Love

Do not trade your magnificent destinies

For the superficial comforts

Of condominiums and vacations

My sisters we are the question and answer of Life

My sisters say yes to your pride

Here Erin is suddenly aware of something

Parker's brush

Hesitating

So she breaks it off

Thanking him for his gift

This time a beautiful Dutch wedding dress

She dresses quickly and descends the stairs

Quoting Duchamp with her Beatle boots

Then out to the infinite possibilities of the Haight

To test her exquisite new powers

Crashpad

A block down from Haight on Ashbury

The Diggers start the Revolution with a free crashpad

Where hippie pilgrims from across America

Can lay their wondrous frazzled bodies down

Dessy gives them flowers and pillows

With a bronzy smile that says Welcome We Love You

Roll out your sleeping bags and make it in the shadows

You've found the safest place in the World to stay

The Diggers embrace and feed your Freedom

What's your name and last mailing address?

Later

When the grass and guitars come out

Dessy makes the rounds

Handing out fresh donuts and cheerful counsel

Her bright eyes photographing every young face

A Pipe Feeding Strawberry Creek

With the serpentine logic of stubborn intellect

Hardy sticks to his plan

Shacking up with women until he feels the evil eye

This time he's busted for taking the last yogurt in the fridge

Back at the Student Union with his little book

Hoping for a lap between the lines

When he realizes he's hit the gap

Sometimes the salt runs eight or nine moves deep

And the center of the board is a black hole

So he hikes up Northside hoping something warm

Will present itself at Giant Burger

But it's a bad night in cardboard

Rousted twice from suitable stoops

Sleepily evading the maniacs of the night

He finds a redwood plank in a dumpster behind GTU

That fits perfectly in a pipe feeding Strawberry Creek

Rejoicing in his privacy

He smokes some shag

And relaxes into dusty dreams

Flowing with the academic drainwater

After a day's foraging a foam cushion

Some silvered industrial insulation

And King Lear to read by flashlight

Hardy's confidence returns

He feels aphorisms growing in his fingernails

And starts thinking romantically again

At The Bear's Lair one bright Berkeley morning

He meets Tina stealing a danish

And hits the jackpot

She's a chess groupie at Hardcastle's

She's got a baggie of Panama Red

In a rakish swoon lasting two weeks

Hardy gets his stuff from the pipe and moves in

They're getting it on seven eight times a day

But when the grass is gone

She asks for a jackson and it's over

He's walking around the carillon tower

Calling Tina Tina

Her creative play with the Sicilian Defense

Her counter-attacking thighs

Then he resigns and wanders over to Strawberry Creek

To check out his old sanctuary

The opening's cemented in

Defended by a neon orange steel grate

And covered with fat purple graffiti worms

As Hardy contemplates the sacrifice of shaving

Three words catch his eye

A twist of history

A literary memorial

Hardy Was Here

A Distinguished Guest

Dessy's talking to her father in Miami

When Emmett Grogan shows up at the door

So you're the Cuban girl who's got it together he says

Shielding a distinguished guest with his overcoat

I hear you're doing a great job with the pad

Keep your name out of the papers and you'll be fine

Tonight we have the pleasure of a psychedelic actor

Who goes by the Digger name of Emmett Grogan

On her yellow legal pad Dessy writes Tim Leary

And follows the antagonistic men into the space

They're arguing about the Bread And Puppet Theater

Punctuating their replies with jigs and Astaire slides

In her eyes Leary's the more accomplished dancer

Leaping like a leprechaun over the sleeping bags

Stooping like a frog and croaking to the young hippies

Turn On Tune In And Drop Out

Then bounding merrily away

Emmett's improvising a mix of pantomime and two-steps

Keeping an imaginary cord of disdain attached to his guest

The runaway audience is clapping a rock and roll rhythm

Tim gliding on the wax of his counterculture celebrity

Emmett giving away a bit of his Being with every spin

When Dessy smacks the floor with black flamenco boots

Hushing the crowd with swirling white and crimson skirts

Shouting gypsy curses to a Spanish melody

Then wisely joining Tim and Emmett for a grand finale

The kids whistle and cheer in happy stoned surprise

As the trio steps into a series of polished Broadway poses

And closes with a barbershop version

Of America The Beautiful

At the door

Dessy thinks Emmett's the more charismatic leader

His heart and self-deception

Would make a great American novel

Your success will be the end of everything

Tim says to her with a wink

After Haight dies

Our only solution will be immigration to the stars

The Winning Streak

They're playing early speed at Bay Meadows

Wheeling every claimer with an X on the form

To third and fourth favorites in the mud

Then dipping over the hill to Half Moon Bay

To party at the half-Italian restaurant behind the biker bar

The streak starts every morning at I-HOP on University

With two eggs over easy and sandpaper muffins

Chased by a bottomless thermos of bad coffee

Frank slouching in his Harris Tweed hunting jacket

Toby in his brown Australian raingear

They're looking for picks with blue magic markers

Same booth same time

Same Macanudo cigar for the Mexican busboy

Twenty-nine cigars and twenty-nine wins

It's raining hard in the cramped parking lot

Frank rolling his boxer shoulders

Toby fingering his waxed moustache

They climb into Frank's white on white Caddy

Feeling itchy caffeine addle their eyes

Something stinks in here

Says Toby at the tollbooth

Might be a dead cat says Frank

Lots of dead cats in Berkeley

Cruising by Candlestick Park

Nobody wants to break the lucky routine

Smells deader than a dead cat

Well it could be Jackson

They let it go until they hit San Mateo

It's Jackson all right

Somewhere between a porno dream and a prison nap

Maybe it's the ski parka

Maybe he brushed his teeth

Toby's Midwestern humor

They leave him in the car

Joining the punters headed for the gates

First stop the saddling paddocks

Looking for bandages or foam

Then a quick check of early money on the tote

Before taking up their usual post at the sixteenth pole

Their pick in the first takes a slim lead to the stretch

Drifts wide and slams the outside rail

The boys are double-checking exacta bets for the second

When Frank spots a familiar face uptrack

What's Bukowsky doing so far north?

He's Hollywood Park

Toby takes a swig of his silver flask

The second race is a bust

Their two picks never get a call

They're gnawing their cigars

When they see Jackson approach the poet

Passing a fat wad of twenties and fifties

Bukowsky spreads the bills

Handing back a healthy cut

Under a blue plastic tent

A pale man cranks a Bolex

The boys are mighty distracted

After the third is official

Jackson gives Bukowsky a bigger stack

The poet jamming his pants pockets full

And letting the rest ride

His pockmarked face a lantern of contentment

The boys skip the fourth and blow the fifth

A cavalry charge for maiden four-year old fillies

She breaks well

Stalking the leaders deep into the stretch

Then quietly pulls up lame

Frank's cursing

When a drunken roar gets his attention

Bukowsky's stomping in wild spirals

Grabbing parkas with fat post office hands

Jackson's split with his cash

No tickets no camera no tent

And so the winning streak ends

They're sitting at the half-Italian restaurant

Eating overcooked spaghetti with clam sauce

Toasting number 29

That Jackson's a chigger in your ass says Toby

Who was the guy with the Bolex?

Touting poets is as low as it gets

Frank's nodding when a police chopper lands on their skulls

Actually it's a white Harley with Rikki and Erin

Popping wheelies as they prance around the pool tables

Taunting the Hell's Angels over their shots

A monster rev in neutral

Then Rikki blows out the bar doors

Taking one off its hinges

They never get back to their food

Dimple replaces the wine

What was that?

Strange day a very strange day says Frank

Might be time to change tracks says Toby

The signs are everywhere

Yes!

Did you see the beauty hanging on?

To Be Hip

Far from the shipping lanes of Eisenhower affluence

The Beats invented hip as a desert island

Where they could discuss existential waves

And the jazz of topical hungers

To be hip was the acme of Being

To know someone at the Paris Review

To wear black turtlenecks and fishnet stockings

To invent a love of poetry that burned

And an underground that howled in triumphant pain

Listening to Monk ramble crazy on the keys

Or Miles Davis stretch the horn

Watch Pollock and DeKooning chop it up

And park abstraction behind expression

To be hip they smoked French cigarettes

And played African finger drums in North Beach

They wore black and thought black

Black was the quintessence of hip

But when Leary brought acid to Harvard

And Ken Kesey took the Merry Pranksters on the road

Life came in colors and hip was square

Sex with LSD made black obsolete

You didn't need free jazz or French Bordeaux

When you had a pretty girl and Owsley acid

The hippies reinvented hip as a wild continent

As the rock of the Revolution

They brought St. George's Hill to the Haight

And adopted the New Law of Righteousness

They watched others as if they were watching themselves

They loved others as if they were loving themselves

They dug the World's common ground

But the Diggers were torched in the grip of winter

By villagers jealous of their healthy pigs

Parson Platt killed Winstanley with the old laws of privilege

The tried and true English rules of brutality and hypocrisy

So if the hippies want to survive Shark

They'll need to keep their women and publications discrete

And learn what the Beats were saying with black

The Day He Beat Bobby Fischer

Frank and Toby are discussing Altizer's radical theology

In Toby's warm Northside apartment

When Hardy shows up with a cold pizza proposition

I got a guy in Lubbock selling primo Acapulco for $20 a kilo

And a dealer in Columbus hot to buy at $450 a pound

My girlfriend's fronting the cash and the connections

You'll never see a deal as sweet as this

The Cuban with the button nose?

Toby fixes a Thai joint with a twist of spit

And it's on

He trots out his Goodwill suitcase

With the sniffproof latex liner

As Frank watches rain skew the Berkeley night

Thinking he has better things to do

We should clear fifteen grand says Toby

Tracing the hitch route on the map

With a stubby green marker

Ornette Coleman bopping on the stereo

Eighteen twenty grand easy

Two material pilgrims heavy with halfpints of Dimple

Hit the University Avenue onramp next morning

With $46 in their pockets

And seven memorized phone numbers

Toby looking the English squire

And Hardy a prophet for hire

They get lucky fast

Elderly couple from Olympia relocating to Phoenix

Say they can sit in the Studebaker Golden Hawk

They're towing behind the RV

After Arizona it gets weird

A psycho eating peanuts picks them up in Santa Fe

Says they're perfect replacements

For the boys that ran away

They're at a donut shop still sweating

When blonde twins wearing yellow hot pants

Ask them to help out with the Swedish movies

They're making at auntie's house on Boundary Street

They're introduced to the rosy boas on the waterbed

And the boys are seriously considering a change of plans

When Hardy overhears Lilly tell Lolly

She wants a gold locket with a four-leaf clover

To celebrate her fourteenth birthday

They're winded at the Los Cruces Greyhound Station

Sitting on the suitcase with tickets to Lubbock

When in walks Brownsville Butch the oilman

Who owns a minority share of Best Western Motels

And has a gold passkey to prove it

They spend three weeks in Oklahoma City eating ribs

And drop back to Lubbock when Butch gets busted

The primo weed is gone so they settle for generic skunk

At twice the price

They thumb from West Texas to Columbus

To find the dealer won't touch the stuff

A phone call to Dessy introduces the backup plan

After chicken and dumplings with Uncle Ralph in Kent

Hardy and Toby hitch to New York

And the Marshall Chess Club

Where Hardy gets a game with Marcel Duchamp

Exchanging down so he can watch the dance of kings

The artist has studied with such arcane precision

The gesture doesn't go unnoticed by the members

And the boys are accepted

Allowed to sleep on the gray velvet cushions

Behind the movable screens

And eat chicken salad sandwiches free

It's 3 on a Thursday afternoon

When purple haze in the Tournament Room

Says Bobby Fischer's here

He's giving 1-5 minute odds at blitz

Moving his long fingers over the pieces like a concert pianist

Hardy goes to the restroom

And forty minutes later Bobby has his zipper down

I've got some killer weed

Might help your mom's insomnia

Fischer gives Hardy a stare to curdle marrow

But reconsiders

His mother hasn't slept since the cops beat her

The day she chained herself to the United Nations Building

So he says OK tomorrow

I need the cash in thirty minutes or no deal

After Bobby splits Hardy goes to the basement

Where he's prepared a pigeon drop

How sweet

The greatest chess player of all time

The American who stood against sixty Russian grandmasters

Reduced to a pawn in the game of Life

Suddenly he has a rush of empathy

Accompanied by a sharp twinge of fear

Can Dessy be playing me for a fool?

I'm nothing compared to Fischer

When do I become the goat?

But the feeling fades on the stained white tiles

Waiting for interlopers to flush and go

Bobby enters with five minutes to spare

Passing Hardy an envelope of crisp fifties

Hardy rips him a corner of the package

Holding out a bud

Bobby sniffs

Nods

1-0

What?

Hardy smiles serene

It's a drop man

He pulls out the shredded newspaper

And tosses the package to the corner

Thinking today's the day I won Dessy's Love

Today's the day I beat Bobby Fischer

He flashes Bobby the peace sign

And hands him the battered suitcase of shag

Good

Good job Dessy says in his head

After Bobby storms out cursing Jews

Fischer's a Russian spy

You'll remember this day the rest of your life

Now reach out and stop the clock

Five-Mile Beach

Rikki's hitting sand shots on The Esplanade

Aiming for a fork of driftwood fifteen yards away

When she spots Sammy coming up lost in thought

And invites him to try the long bunker shot

She sees something right in this reserved outlaw

And the perimeter defenses to her heart fall

When Sammy hits his first ball inside the circle

They pass an hour hitting long explosions

And collecting strays in her black Titleist bag

After long minutes of taut and telling silence

Sammy kisses her with unmistakable concern

Her first impulse is to crush his thorax

But a second melts a hard young life to tears

And she returns his unasked questions with breathlessness

Surrendering her martial training to his desire

They embrace beside Mover's Service

Kissing cautiously

Blown away by a sudden gale

Into a dream they never knew they were having

Everything they did before

Brought them to this beach

Everybody they knew before

Brought them to this touch

Everything surreal and slow

Then hyperreal and racing

As the World matches their vaulting temperature

And tender accelerations

They drive up Lincoln to pick up her things

Skipping down the Digger steps

Her Wilson Staffs rattling in a canvas carry bag

They're clear of The City by late afternoon

He's talking about his graduate studies in physics

How UCSC ignored his new thermodynamic model

How the strongest force in the universe

Is the repulsive force of emptiness

She's silent on Nam

The ease of their privacy reminding them

There's nothing to do

They're deeply in love

Rolling down Highway 1 in clipped horizontal light

Letting the moment command

Stopping at Five Mile Beach to check out the choppy waves

Screwdrivers in plastic cups jumping starfish puddles

Briefly touching barely moving then scrambling over rocks

They decide to have another drink stay the night

Rikki tenses as time approaches

She's ready for anything

But mostly she doesn't want this magic to pass

Neither does he

And they fall asleep in their clothes

Listening to the coastal crickets

Shortly before dawn Sammy tools the van into Santa Cruz

Picks up some blueberry muffins and coffee

They're parked under the giant oak

Behind the tenth green at Pasatiempo Golf Club

Waiting for the sun to fight through the fog

Keen to play a match on MacKenzie's track

They sky their drives on 11

Lose their approaches in the barranca

Chip close for pars on the dogleg 12th

Their short putts leaving snailtracks on the dewy green

As steam rises from the warming fairways

Rikki birdies 13 to go one-up

Sammy answers with a thirty-footer on 14

They both par the short par 3

And come to the famous 16th all-square

Rikki leaks her drive into the black oaks

Then powerfades a three-iron stiff

Sammy hits a soft draw to the garden spot

Then airmails a seven-iron over the green

That catches the slope and goes OB

He drops a ball and does it again

He's standing by his bag

Watching Rikki putt out

When two police cruisers stop

Get your ID says the young cop with a military cut

His partner covering with a double-barreled shotgun

As Sammy bends to get his license

The cop clubs him on the head

No fake ID Dr Groom?

You took my grandmother for five grand

And now it's payback time

He kicks Sammy with steel-tipped boots

Rikki's charging

Inches from the cop's neck

When the vet catches her temple with blue steel

She screams and drops

Cold

The old cop takes a closer look motions the rookie away

This is trouble this is the bitch

That threw Randy from the balcony of The Tea Cup

The one that beat up Indian Tom in the riverbed

And killed the second Doberman with the carcass of the first

When a Columbian hitman found her on the mall

It's time we did our rounds come on

They're trash

Nobody cares if they're dead

Come now

Rikki wakes first

Five ten minutes later

Calling softly for Sammy

Ranger training collects the bags

And carries her man to the van

Not knowing the severity of his concussion

Retreat is her first priority

She's headed back up Highway 1 thinking of switching cars

When Sammy comes to moaning and cursing

She pulls to the shoulder and checks him out

He's got a bad lump he'll be fine

They're headed to Five Mile Beach

Eating peanut butter sandwiches drinking screwdrivers

Escaping Death together has done it

They park where they parked before

And now it's time

Finally time

For the bittersweet transcendence

Of pure sex

The Elevators At Langley Porter

The elevators are beyond the palms

Says the nightclerk through his doublemint

But you're better off taking the stairs

He adds with a bucktooth leer

Jackson shuffles over in his horseblanket

Accompanied by his invisible orderly Tatarugu

Watching the floor numbers light and dim

The doors cranking slipping

Then hissing open to reveal a lush burgundy décor

Hello you've got a nice set of cowlicks

Says hawkfaced Dr Groom amiably

Sizing up the potential of his new patient

If you've read the story by Buzzati

You'll appreciate our modest improvements

He scans the floppy admittance forms

Trying to attract Jackson's attention

With a series of professional clicks

But Jackson's replaying his evening

The final dinner with picayune architects

Marzipan dessert spilled on the silk tablecloth

The howling ghost of Artaud

Claiming he can't get no satisfaction

So Jackson decides to hang the albatross

And voluntarily commit himself to a nuthouse

The cabbie wants a story so he tells the one

About Joshua Norton

Who called himself Emperor of America

And claimed all the land from St Louis to San Francisco

The Emperor would trade ten thousand acres for a steak dinner

A Nevada City mining claim for a young whore

When the Texas Rangers got close he disappeared

Into the Grand Canyon of his mind

Some say he turned Indian

Took squaws that smelled of juniper and pitch

Some think the Emperor of America

Became our alternate history

Trading the idea of Dominion for a night in a feather bed

Jackson wasn't particularly bored or distressed

He thought of it as good breeding

What every Southern gentleman should do

What Aeschylus predicted

The psychic exchange of Manifest Destiny

For free room and board in a five-star asylum

It takes two hours for the elevator

To get to the Seventh Floor

Where Jackson is checked in

Strapped to TV and IV

And encouraged to count commercials on his fingers

He's eating extremely well

He's grown a Viennese accent and a thick moustache

He's accompanying Dr Groom on his rounds

And then with the supreme directness of Life

He's Dr Groom on his rounds

His political strength is the social calendar

Weekly dances for patients and staff

Culminating in Nazi Hula Night

When he's promoted down to the Fifth Floor

And personally nominated by the Director

To give the annual lecture

To the Insurance Underwriters Of America

Reich was always on track

He intones from the double-breasted podium

But he missed two big deltas

Which we now know to be profit and homoeroticism

The generosity of the applause enables Dr Groom

To loosen his tie

Gentlemen Langley Porter has shown Freud the door

And irrefutably demonstrated

To the International Scientific Community

That male mental disease can by cured by turning gay

Our patients are taken to the Turkish Baths south of Market

And the glory holes of Castro Street twice a week

The underwriters stomp as he rolls out the numbers

88% of our patients need no further treatment

After two years only 7% have any detectable mental disease

Gentlemen there is no hospital or clinic in the world

With numbers like these

We take America's lunatics and turn them into lambs

So Langley Porter fully merits your upgrade to A plus

More clapping and stomping

Groom! Groom! Groom!

In the echoes of thunderous applause

The transition of kings is complete

Dr Groom decorates his new Third Floor office

With Warhol prints

And starts renting out the elevators

To charity-minded civic groups

Political action committees and cloaked corporations

For a flat fee of $3000 an hour

It's quickly the hottest fundraiser in The City

With the Policemen's Benevolent Society booked solid

From 10-4 Friday and Saturday nights

And Dr Groom skimming four or five grand a day

Plus a grand for the specialty videos

He runs out to The Tenderloin

Everything's rolling with Wagnerian grandeur

When someone in City Hall discovers

His social security number

Belongs to a Mexican infant

Who couldn't survive a day in Lodi

So he's busted before making First Floor

The Langley Porter staff takes up a collection

For a Halloween Ball

A skeleton dance in the lobby

With the Charlatans and Blue Cheer

Tatarugu lets out a loud and mournful howl

As the Director awards Dr Groom

The Crown Of Permanent Sanity

And whispers a personal request in his ear

Like Napoleon leaving for Elba he closes his eyes

Touches his balls

And becomes James Brown

Singing Please Please Please

Emerging from the zebraskin cape

Cakewalking backwards to the steel doors of Langley Porter

And disappearing into the night

In My Arms

Remember your blood Chica Mia

You're the daughter of a cop

The granddaughter of a detective

And a Cardoza never questions the rules

That hold Christian society together

When we were poor in Havana

We never allowed philosophy in the house

And every shirt your mother washed

Every punk dealer I busted

Brought us one step closer to America

I understand your self-doubt

Things are dirty in San Francisco

And undercover work is always tough

It's easy to heat the role

And melt into the enemy's lines

So remember Chica

Emmett Grogan

Peter Berg

And the Diggers

Are Communist threats to America

Tom Hayden and the New Left are splintered

Well infiltrated and unfit to organize the unions

The Black Panthers are suicides

Laughed at by their own people

But behind the makeshift masks of street theater

The Diggers have created terrorist cells

Designed to destroy our liberty

They want to kick your mother out of her house

So their homeless friends can move in

They denounce our public law of nuisance

They refuse to present demands to elected officials

They prefer to steal what they want

And give it away to the poor

Your mission is to discredit them in the hippie counterculture

Dismember and destroy them

If their ideas of common property

And psychological emancipation

Spread to the middle class

Riots will come to Chicago Memphis LA

And demonic fire will leap to every ghetto mind

We have a plan Chica

For the future of America and the World

Dallas was a demonstration of our deep political power

But it also exposed a flawed strategy

Now we strike every Evil before it matures

Haight-Ashbury must fall

Once domestic hippie resistance is crushed

We can subvert the economies of Russia and China

With counterfeit money and luxury goods

Once we secure global oil resources

And establish permanent American military bases

In key arenas

Communism will die

And a New American Empire will be born

Dessy

You are the Chosen One

God commands you to bring Peace to the World

God commands you to kill the Diggers

Keep to the fundamentals you learned at Miami Academy

And you'll be OK

Your mother sends her Love

And prays for you every night

Keep your gun well oiled

And never skip target practice

The Diggers are psychotics

Highly skilled in propaganda and mind control

Remember that intelligence or compassion

Takes you straight into their traps

Don't answer their questions

Don't ask any yourself

You are Good

You are the Chosen One

This is all you need to know

You're dealing with Satanists and Communists

One day you'll need to defend yourself with total force

Trust Security

Trust your instincts

Defend yourself

And call us from the Mission Street Station

On our regular schedule

Don't underestimate the Diggers Chica Mia

They have the silver tongues of Satan

And the Hegelian logic of his infernal seed

They're more dangerous for America

Than racial integration or nuclear proliferation

So think of me when it gets tough

Remember when you were two

And I held you in my arms for fifty hours

Crossing to Florida in that small fishing boat

If you don't eliminate the Diggers

If you get into drugs or free sex

If you fail this mission

I'll drop you into the sea Dessy

And disown you as a Cardoza

Mother is adamant

You know she is

If you flip out and become a hippie

Don't call or try to come home

If you're troubled

Spend more time at the target range

Review the fundamentals

And remember that with every victory and promotion

We love you more

Fruitvale

The third car's broken down on McArthur

So the second has to cover its own ass tonight

It's bad attitude as the Black Panthers patrol Oakland

Barbeque baby back ribs hanging from the bone

On August stoops steaming with summer race

Extra hot sauce wash it down with Keystone beer

And paper plates of anonymous white bread

Huey Newton drives the point through Fruitvale

Flashing his million-dollar smile to the corner shooters

Stopping at every raucous group of cornrow kids

To throw out Snickers bars from a Safeway bag

Remember to show up for drills he tells the girls

Self-defense is your only way to Black Power

Huey's working his turf like a Southern politician

Handing out black berets to scowls in afros

And grinning at Parker's Pentax

Aimed from the trailing Ford

Bob Dylan and Joan Baez were in my studio yesterday

Parker tells Bobby Seale at the wheel

Sang Your Cheatin Heart

One prize memory

Swept away by Huey's Fruitvale

Playing out ahead

What's going down?

Bobby continues to ignore him

They're tracking Oakland Cruiser #33

With Ornutt and Carpenter on the sheet

When they stumble into a 7-11 robbery

Three police cruisers block the parking lot

Sending technicolor shadows into the sweat

Huey smoothes his hoppedup Riviera past the scene

Stopping two blocks up on Harrison

Bobby jumps the curb into some weeds

Slipping on his Italian kidskin gloves

Huey ambles over

Toothpick twitching from his lower lip

They load shotguns in stony silence

What do we do with the tourist?

Huey murmurs something and splits

Bobby counts fifty slow raps on the dash

And disappears down an alley

From the wet backseat

Parker sees the ghetto war coming down

He bolts from the car looking for cover

An Arco station explodes

Blasting balls of fire over the surrounding houses

He finds shelter in an old garage

Stinking fifty years of oil changes and chickenshit

He hides behind empty boxes

Slumping in a stack of tires

His penis hard from fantasy

And the violence of constant observation

After twenty thirty minutes

Huey and Bobby slip in

Their shotguns pointed up safari style

Joking about the new photograph

J Edgar Hoover in drag

Another explosion

Maybe the 76 station over on Union

Parker wants to say something

But he drops off

Waking or dreaming four hours later

The full moon falling through broken glass

Makes a bright circle for a little Black girl

Her hair spiked in shiny exclamations

Holding a Barbie and a bread knife

You're a bad bad Barbie

I found you and gave you cookies

I gave you tea every day at 4

I taught you how to walk and how to talk

I fought for you

I wrote poems for you

I loved you and you betrayed me

You burned down my house!

What's going to happen to me now?

You stupid Barbie!

You stupid bad bad Barbie!

She cuts its head off

And kicks it into the darkness

What's going to happen to me now?

Now that I know?

Now that I know that I know?

Dig The Diggers

Peter Berg's pacing midnight

Holding a flashlight tight under his chin

Chanting theater theory

At a meeting of the Diggers Board

We've created the conditions we describe

Dig the Diggers

We give homes to the homeless

Dig the Diggers

We give clothes to the naked

Dig the Diggers

We give soup to the hungry

Dig the Diggers

We are the actors and the chorus of our time

Dig the Diggers

And if anybody wants to know who our leader is?

Emmett Grogan!

Again

Emmett Grogan!

And if anybody wants to know who Emmett Grogan is?

We are!

Dig The Diggers!

Dig The Diggers!

Our gig is social action

Dig The Diggers

Our style is New Righteousness

Dig The Diggers

We take what we want think what we want

Love who we want leave who we want

Dig The Diggers

We don't need Vietnam we don't need America

Dig The Diggers

We are The Frame Of Reference

Dig The Diggers

We are the end of Private Property

Dig The Diggers

We are the beginning of Life as Art

Dig The Diggers

We are Free Men!

Dig The Diggers!

Who are we?

Emmett Grogan!

Dig The Diggers!

Dig The Diggers!

Cool

Now we have some business for the Board

America's hippies are flooding Haight-Ashbury

If we can't reinvent the City

Or provide basic social services

The Revolution is lost

So with complete confidence

We've appointed Dessy our Coordinator

You know her dedication to the crashpad

She's our Mary our Desdemona our Kuan Yin

When your founders are eating crayfish

She'll be building the Free Clinic

The Free Store

The Free Bank

And the other institutions we need for a Free City

So Emmett and I want you to understand

Dig the Diggers!

Whatever Dessy thinks we think

Dig the Diggers!

Whatever she plans we plan

Dig the Diggers!

My friends we've seen many changes

Since the early days of the Mime Troupe

In this midnight hour

In this old Victorian

We too must become the conditions we describe

We are the Diggers

We dig the Soil

We dig the Spirit

We dig the Intellect

We dig the Revolution

We ignore the War

We ignore the Police

We ignore the Law

We dig Art

We dig Life

Dig the Diggers!

We introduce New Sense to a mad world

Dig the Diggers!

But are you willing to sacrifice your Life for Art?

Peter flashes light in a handsome face

Are you?

And you?

Are you willing to sacrifice your Death for these kids?

Dig the Diggers!

Someone in here is a cop

Dig the Diggers!

Somebody knows what we're doing

Even as we conceal it from ourselves

Dig the Diggers!

Leap through the Frame of Reference!

Our moment onstage is brief

And Emmett Grogan's is briefer yet

So dig the Diggers while you can

Spread enlightenment in every smile

Become who you are

Instantly

Without work or pain

Instantly

Without searing desire

Instantly

Like a flashlight turning off

Instantly

Like this

The Curtains

Sammy jumps the low iron fence

And takes the granite steps slowly

His meeting with Billy

Rattling in his head like loaded dice

He wanders the lawn above Berkeley's Greek Theater

Remembering Purple Barrel tennis matches

Played with phosphorescent balls in Scarsdale

And finished with cream sodas at the diner

The transatlantic rendezvous at Delphi

Billy's Orange Sunshine flying from New York

Sammy's hitching down from Thebes

Thunder rolling a clear sky at 1

In divine approval of their punctuality

The Silver Dome appointment in Devonshire

Billy taking a cab from London

Sammy by boat and train from Cologne

Spooking survivalists in the darkling trees

Evading a pack of hungry children

With missing noses and ears

To find relief in tumblers of Glenmorangie

Now Sammy sees his friend

The Poe forehead and pallor

The fresh red bandana and faded jeans

Leaning casual against the stage

Discussing the virtues of tall women with Daffy Duck

As Sammy surfs down the concrete shell

To meet where the acoustics are best

Two uninvited questions arise

Am I protected?

Am I doomed?

Billy's gone

And Sammy's possessed by iridescent white curtains

Hanging from the tall Ionic columns

Watching them billow and fill billow and fill

He feels the salty presence of Aphrodite

He feels her dress touching his cheek

And one question is answered

Hexagrams

After a mean lunch of coke and Quaaludes

Erin's looking into the mirror with a razor

Listening to Tim Buckley on the stereo

Thinking cut three Chinese hexagrams

Break the terrible symmetry of my beauty

And the market it makes wherever I go

She swings the blade close to her right breast

Thinking slice it off Amazon style

So I can shoot straighter with a bow

Knowing if she allows this mood to fester she's lost

She digs out Tom Hayden's number from her purse

And calls the Red Family on the hot line

Remembering his pink political flattery in bed

It's busy probably tapped

She's quickly dressed driving on the Bay Bridge

The seagulls calling her name

She needs something and doesn't know what it is

Missing the Telegraph turn she finds herself at 2793

Parked numb in front of Feather's house

She nods to Toby at the desk

So lost she finds the rough cotton thread

Leading down the long cedar hallway

To Feather's white pine bed

You're getting fat

She says starting to cry

You're Rahab

I've never done this before

I'm not just another dyke in a pickup

Feather sings softly

There is only Love

There is no Hate

There is only Love

There is nothing to gain

There is nothing to lose

We are One

You are here to see yourself

You are here to love yourself

You are here to be Me

There is only Love

There is no Hate

We are One

There is only Love

We are Me

We are One

And One is always One

There is only Love

There is no Hate

We are Me

We are One

And One is always One

The Jack Of Spades

Frank's writing his novel in Room 218

Playing The Key Club

To cover $85 a week rent

And keep his mind sharp

Until the book's done

It's a classic cowboy table

Five card draw

Quarter ante table stakes

He controls Jake The Rake

Kingfish Barrington and the other pros

He knows their moves and tells so well

Their hands are translucent

It's just a matter of position fresh fish

And bluffing enough to keep the table on tilt

He plays until dawn

Walks carefully across McArthur

For a quart of Rainier at Rollie's Liquor

A double cheeseburger at the Doggie Diner

Then breakfast back in his room

Surrounded by black orchid wallpaper

And work in progress

He's writing on the JFK assassination

He's got the Cuban connection

The Mafia motive

The Pentagon memos to Johnson

He knows which America died

And what monster born

He's got a secret society hidden in plain sight

But he's trapped in his own game

If he's hot he has to play because he's hot

If he's salty he has to play to pay the rent

His life's become a day job

Passed off as literature

The poker hands never quit

And the book never comes around

Buried in routine he walks out afternoons

Up San Pablo to the Sunny Café

For three eggs over easy with grits

Imagination and determination crowd his mind

Their intricate cover stories

Mocking and dislodging crucial memories

He's looking for a sign to get out

It's a rainy night in Emeryville

The Key Club bar big with truckers and hookers

There's an action hand at the back table

With six raises before the draw

Frank's got aces-up with the bug

He figures Jake The Rake for a baby full

And Kingfish for a big flush

He does the right thing at the wrong time

Discarding the queen of spades

Convinced he needs a big boat to win

He catches the jack of spades

Giving him a royal flush in the hand he trashed

So now he's tapped out

Watching from furious distance

As Barrington lays down the four deuces

He slowplayed by the book

Convinced a two-grand mistake

Can tell the Truth

Frank's sitting in the night chill

On the busbench he often derided

When he was catching cards

Feeling a soft stab of relief

Poker's over

His novel's gone with the room

He's free

The rebel Owen Glendover

Overcomes the actor and spy

It seems the first bus he ever saw

The friendliest driver

After Central Terminal he finds a great cup of coffee

And starts walking towards the Haight

Daybreak finds him on the Panhandle

Sharing granola with a runaway from Iowa City

The jack was his last draw

That life's over

He's a hippie now

The Luckiest Day Of His Life

Erin's tired of Sartre and subterfuge

Sick of enterprise and isolation

She decides to go looking for Rikki

Her slim friend on the white Harley

She met moons ago down the coast

She dresses in tan shorts and a halter top

A bright blue Indian silk scarf flowing

Elephant sandals and minimal makeup

She drives out to Golden Gate Park

Calling Rikki to the Japanese Tea Garden

She parks her car near Strawberry Hill

And wanders over to the Polo Field

Feeling the hot sun lick her alabaster skin

Watching small groups of hippies dancing

Frisbee dogs chasing and jumping

Her eyes drawn to a husky boy

With a curly red mane and Grateful Dead t-shirt

Patting the flanks of a shaggy black mutt

Realizing she's staring she turns away

But then he's standing there

Sweating and catching his breath

You're the most beautiful woman in the world

I saw you in a biker bar in Half Moon Bay

May I know the name of my bride?

Erin nods

I'm Frank and this is Heraclitus

We were reunited this morning

After a year and four hundred miles

Now he's got green paint and a taste for Frisbees

And I've got long hair and a taste for freedom

We understand each other perfectly

Always have

So allow me to introduce myself again

I'm Frank and I've done a few things

I've been present during the World's Absence

And absent during the World's Presence

I've written a bit and been booked a bit

The CIA and the KGB are both looking for me

And this is the luckiest day of my life

My wife and dog so well met

So well met

Heraclitus barks

Offering a slobbery blue disc

Frank fakes twice then flings it hard

He's my mentor and you're my Muse

I'm looking for someone

She has to say something

She hates his tie-dyed t-shirt and scruffy beard

She's temporizing like mad

I think I know who it is

Rikki's a Digger now

Helps Emmett serve soup in the Panhandle

Every afternoon at 4

I really have to go

I have an appointment

She's fiddling with her blue silk purse

When Frank sees her as Caridwen

Bathed in ancient Welsh rays of lunar adoration

Calling his white stag to the thicket

Heraclitus bouncing alert

Yes boy meet your new mistress

This is Erin

She'll be with us forever

She knows the source and purpose of this moment

She'll be his Triple Goddess until his poem arrives

His inspiration until her double-axe falls

Come on boy let's find her friend

Walking towards the Mustang

They're captured by the singing mud of Metson Lake

Splashing down as the newest heirs of Mother Earth

Mentally touring their great and enigmatic domain

Watching seaweed sweep the sky

Frank feels a doubt arise

Could this girl be Straight?

So he traces a thick brown arrow on his arm

And dedicates his new Life to her happiness

Thinking as the World rages and changes

Surely a man deserves a lucky day like this

Poppies

Heraclitus chasing purple butterflies

Through fields of electric orange poppies

As Frank and Erin stroll wet Muir Woods trails

Their hands fainting at the slightest loss of contact

Their minds thrilling to a new double identity

Erin's spitting out recent New York visuals

Auditioning for Andy Warhol at The Factory

In overheated lofts of aluminum foil and talcum power queens

Andy says Death is chic everybody is doing Death

You're the next Superstar

You're everything the World wants

Then three sharp barks and she's back

Leaning her head on Frank's shoulder

Crying for joy

Free Food

Rikki's gutted the Ford van

And put up a security screen behind the seats

Every run they make is timed to the second

And she knows how many pounds of beef

Will fill up the back how fast

They range from Sonoma to San Jose

Hitting the major wholesalers early morning

Sometimes with a fake accident blocking traffic

When Rikki wears a dress and falsies

But usually something semi-automatic

Works to shake down the drivers

Every score is affirmation of Digger philosophy

Take what you need without ideology or negotiation

They want beef for the hippies in the Haight

So they take it from the belly of American Straight

From Safeway loading docks in Fremont Daly City

From boats of Argentinean tenderloin

From the pantries of the best hotels

Dressed in sharp suits and uniforms from the Free Store

The skinny blonde with the cleft chin

And Jesse James with the glacier blue eyes

They hit the Bay Area with fake plates

Fake lettering and meticulous preparation

The teamsters are usually cool

But not every score is clean

And sometimes the blood is theirs

Rikki leading them out with karate kicks

Driving over dividers and through sirens

To make their afternoon appointment in the Panhandle

They feed two three hundred hippies a day

Setting up milk cans braising the sides

Dropping in carrots celery onions

Pepper and oregano

Without free food the kids are busted

Hounded by cops hustlers or on the bus

Back to Omaha Atlanta San Diego

Watching them spoon beef from the soup

Rikki and Sammy revel in their open secret

Every danger tempers their Love like a samurai sword

The humility of service feeds their romantic pride

This is who they are and what they do

Believing like Marion and her Robin Hood

That Courage

Is the only true Freedom

The Acid Test

Ken Kesey kicks it off

With his Psychedelic Symphonette

And a thousand electric gadgets

Hack and hum with senseless urgency

Nobody can tell what's going on

So everybody tries the acid Kool-Aid

Swirling Concord Grape in a baby bathtub

Kesey prances the Fillmore as The Human Torch

While Neal Cassady juggles a ten-pound hammer

To keep his internal organs tight

A hundred students from Straight classrooms

Watch the Hip teachers with delight

Looking for tips and clues to pass The Acid Test

The word went out two nights ago

And Dessy made sure

Her Digger staff could make the scene

Could see her drinking LSD and eating hash brownies

Catch her belly dancing with her swami consort

Lock these images in

So no new information or discovery

Could ever blow her cover

She's cool

She knows what's happening

Rising above the autistic noise of the Pranksters

She hears The Grateful Dead playing

Sitting On Top Of The World

The kids dig rock and roll

Oblivious to Kesey's intent

She sees Rikki and Sammy slow-dancing

Quoting the Fifties

And the perfect rotation of the planets

She sees Dr Groom and Billy in a contest of wit

Improving a Falstaff monolog

She sees Frank and Erin naked in the strobes

Miming the birth of the Uebermensch

Her team's strong and getting stronger

And Dessy feels the first anticipations of success

She sees herself surprising Dad with dinner at Gino's

Knitting quietly with Mom

As swamp crickets fill the back yard

She's following the flow of Jerry's noodling

When suddenly chill

She sees Hardy edging his way

Toward the yellow Phoenician tent

Taking a step stroking his beard another step

Like a lioness Dessy stalks and times her leap

Hardy falls

His turban cocked

His arms pinned to the floor

Eyes trembling

Feather appears at the flap as brilliant Astarte

So Dessy deftly switches to horseplay

Loudly proclaiming her jealousy

And silently vowing revenge

Feather's too pure to understand

She's angling her bulk inside when everybody stops

Stops everything stops eating stops drinking stops dancing

Stops dreaming just stops

The Goddess of Love has come to the Haight!

Everybody's here!

An electric surge of ecstasy darts and swirls

Through the Fillmore

Everybody feels tight with Feather

Totally in love with a Joyful Wisdom

And the rush of living beyond Good and Evil

Now the crowd's thirsty for Orange Kool-Aid

As Rikki and Sammy embody collective desire

By handing Feather a bouquet of wildflowers

And making love on her sheepskin rug

When the police arrive at 2

Everybody's graduated The Acid Test

Making it with the one they love or the one they're with

On the cliff or in the shadows

The Pranksters and cops

Continue to hassle lights and power plugs

Through the early morning hours

But Dessy's long gone

Taking her Diggers home through the backstage door

Above The Center

You know Shark everything's connected

When you hear everybody talking about Love

You can bet Hate's the root of it

It's all a matter of perception

We're Diggers now

Sitting on the roof of the Digger Free Clinic

Above the corner of Haight and Ashbury

The most famous intersection in history

The Center of Centers as long as we continue to watch

You know I wasn't always Dr Groom

My training was philology

But Dessy trusted my talent

And gave me the Director's white coat

So now I can call a spade a spade

I love Homer

I love Chaucer

I love Shakespeare and Whitman

I love Melville and Beckett

But I hate microbes

I hate our biological ancestors

Because their survival strategies ruin our lives

Our modern psychiatry is filled with these ancient bugs

So I kill bugs with drugs

Free drugs from the Free Clinic

You see how everything matches up?

Most of these kids have strep or clap

From eating bad and living on the street

They learn to hate bugs the hard way

But how did they get to the Haight?

By hating their parents

Hating their teachers

Hating their neighbors

Hating TV

Hating homecoming dances

But mostly they got here by hating Straight America

And its cruel treatment of quick and singular kids

Hate makes them come to Haight-Ashbury looking for Love

And when they find it

They want to love America and their parents again

But now they're hated and disowned by the ones they love

So Love and Hate become fused

And every new affection

Is laced with secret repulsion

Love-Hate is Nature Shark

It's the coincidence of opposites sought by the mystics

It's the unification of forces sought by the physicists

It's out there

And it's in here

Love-Hate links all Being

Everything else is illusion or ignorance

Look at those Russian and American programs

The Nation State had its hooks in you good

Your success was guaranteed

But you saw too much or learned too fast

Maybe went too far East or West

Maybe fell in love with a beautiful girl

Who appeared to fall for you

If she's part of their program

If she betrays you

You say Yes!

If the Revolution fails

You say Yes!

Because tragedy is the vision

That excites creative Will

It's the irrational structure

And goal of all Reason

Love-Hate links all Non-Being

Everything else is illusion or ignorance

And here's where it gets interesting Shark

If Love-Hate links Being to Non-Being

Then the link is the only reality we can know

The World enters and exits

Whenever Love-Hate changes frequency

Think of the fistfight with your father

The day you returned home from Leningrad

I can still see that bright August kitchen

As clearly as I see you now

When my mother broke her favorite Ming vase

On my shoulder

Think of Hardy and his double-entry dad

Feather and her four sets of fosters

Parker's domineering mom

Rikki and The Parents Who Were Always Out To Dinner

Dessy hears these voices

She's so crazy with Hate for her father

She calls him daily in her head

And writes him long letters she burns and flushes

To document two long years of silence

Everything depends on our little runaway now

Emmett and Peter are gone

Headed for the East Village

To spread their Philosophy of Free

By the way Shark you need a little cash?

Couple side things here doing OK

You're still naive when it comes to money

Just because you're director of the Free Bank

And print your own notes doesn't mean you're hip

Your Digger Dollars are a Machiavellian curse

And won't keep friends from your throat when you fall

How long can you keep Erin satisfied?

How long will she wait for a house and garden?

How long will she love you

When she can't see the way to security?

You're Dionysus

You're ethereal creation and chthonic destruction

Your duty is to expand Consciousness

And hate everything semi-conscious that apes your work

You must retool the Homeric epic

Reinvent American poetry

Reverse its dry Apollonian interiors

Refute its academic and ornamental confessions

You must sing of Haight-Ashbury

Bursting from the steel brow of New America

Sing of Emmett

Peter

Dessy

Rikki

The many heroes and heroines of the Revolution

Without singing of yourself

Overflow with the political Will

That unites history and philosophy

Destroy the semi-conscious Apparatus with words!

You're Orpheus

Whitman

You must sing of yourself

Beause if you lose your contradictions

We lose our confidence

And the World unwinds

So what do you think of Dessy now?

Isn't she a Georgia peach?

Before she put things together

The Diggers were a trip by the Mime Troupe

A Dada construct signed with masking tape

She's tightened the message

Broadened the appeal of the hippie counterculture

She started with a basement crashpad

And now we have two blocks of Ashbury

From Haight to the Panhandle

And free services going on all over The City

Emmett and Peter are great but Dessy gets things done

All San Francisco knows she's great copy

She transcends the cant of the HIP merchants

She's brassy like Pearl

Organized like Bill Graham

She's Mary Magdalene on acid

Without her thousands of hippies would go hungry

Or crazy in suburban reformatories

I guess it's time

I can see it in your face

Since I turned gay everything I say has an asterisk

Well I hate men and now I can hate them close

I get inside their hearts twist them mad

And leave them desperate for somebody else

It's my private war

I conduct it for the sole purpose

Of improving my eyesight

Look at those hippies down there

Hustling their next baggie or squeeze

Hate is their master and disaster their game

No matter how fresh the flowers in their hair

We know they'll need penicillin soon

So who's the greater fool Shark?

The smart middle-class kid who believes

He can have Freedom forever

In a new society where everything is cool

Or the rooftop observer who affirms the Revolution

Knowing revolutions are crushed for far less?

The Trips Festival

All gods please come onstage

Kesey projects the invitation on screens

In the Longshoreman's Hall

Backed by sepia slides of Hopi sweathouses

And giant Burmese Buddhas

Two sure spirits venture forward

Then there's five preening and posing in the lights

Venice Beach meets Avatar Night at the Trips Festival

There's Baba Free John and Charles Manson

There's Feather and Huey Newton

There's Timothy Leary and twenty deities nobody knows

It's over a hundred happy incarnations on a small stage

Until the strongest boards break

And the gods leap in the minds of their friends

Peter And Emmett Will Be Back Soon

I want to open with praise for Feather

Dig the Diggers!

Since she's moved in I think everyone can agree

Love's alive in everything we do

Dig the Diggers!

I know for sure my tom has nine lives

Dessy hugs a beaming Hardy and winks to her crew

Rikki and Sammy entwined

Frank and Erin enthused

This is what it's all about my friends

Free Men and Free Women making Free Love

In the Free City of The Haight

With the Diggers providing free beds

Free food free clothes free money free drugs for everybody

Dig the Diggers!

My friends everything is accelerating for a reason

Dig the Diggers!

At the Acid Test I had an idea

What if the Diggers could get the Tribes together?

The Berkeley New Left Tribes

With the Haight Psychedelic Tribes

The Black Panther Tribes with the Hell's Angel Tribes

The American Tribes with the Vietnamese Tribes

My friends I have a vision of A Great Gathering

The Tribes Of Hippies and the Tribes of Straights

Coming together for a Free Be-In

Everyone dancing and singing

Everyone celebrating the great gift of Being

A Human Be-In in Golden Gate Park!

Dig The Diggers!

My friends and fellow Diggers

Peter and Emmett will be back soon

So let's give them a real Digger homecoming

We'll carry the Frame of Reference to a new dimension

Tim Leary and Jerry Rubin will be there

Quicksilver and The Grateful Dead

Dig The Diggers!

Gary Snyder and Allen Ginsberg

Dig The Diggers!

Dig your lovers

Do your own thing!

That's what it's all about

Feather's sleeping now but her spirit lifts us all

Let your hearts fill with gratitude my friends

There's never been a time like this in human history

She's overturning everything based on Hate

Every corrupt political and economic structure

Every fear-driven personal relation

Surrenders to her power of Love

That's what it's all about

What we do as individuals means nothing

If we leave behind an entrenched Police State

An America without hope or critical intelligence

Being Free means taking responsibility

Taking American society beyond the tyranny of Law

And neurotic self-interest

A Digger thinks first of other Diggers

How can I encourage their special talents and destinies?

How can I spark her intellect?

How can I stimulate his talent?

How can I guide our children to a free and healthy future?

Being a Digger means being a defender of Mother Earth

Determined to make the World a healthier place to live

The Be-In will start the healing

Do Johnson and American society hate us?

Dig The Diggers!

Do the Media and politicians ridicule us?

Dig The Diggers!

Do the Christian Churches curse us?

Dig The Diggers!

Dig your lovers!

The Be-in will start the healing

Do your own thing!

Everything we do we do for Love

Peter and Emmett will be back soon

Double Delight

I'm home Mama where's your hat where's your hat?

Parker finds a straw western on a chair

And sets it lightly on his mother's head

As she waters Double Delights in the backyard

You still sewing for the stars Parker?

She doesn't bother to look up

But he can feel her power and control

I did the chicken bones for Janis Joplin

And Bob Dylan's vest for Don't Look Back

Sounds like everybody gets along up north

It's coming to Watts Mama just you wait

Pretty soon there's no White Man Black Man

Everything's gonna start over from scratch

Pretty soon everybody's gonna do their own thing

You mean shirking their responsibilities Parker?

It's gonna be different real soon Mama I promise

Everybody's gonna be proud to be together

So you're not hanging with the Black Panthers any more?

No Mama I joined a social action group called the Diggers

We provide free food and shelter for runaway hippies

Well that sounds a lot more dangerous to me son

Hanging with anarchists is the dumbest thing you can do

Maybe it's time for you to go back and finish high school

Maybe you're still smart enough to cut that mangy afro

They stare at each other knowingly through the roses

I'll cut it when you pose for me in the Haight Mama

In the burgundy cape and gown I gave you last Christmas

Parker pictures her sitting sexy royal on his pine stool

When a cold spurt of water catches him in the face

And they run laughing into the kitchen for pink lemonade

Fillmore And Avalon

Fillmore and Avalon are sacred spaces

The arrows of time come full circle

The moon waxing blue on auditorium walls

Says everything old is new

And every home is here

In a psychedelic fusion of roots and ravishing

Life disarms Death

And claims this waxy wood for dancing

Tonight Bill Graham shares a joint with Chet Helms

R Crumb sketches with Mouse

The Diggers shake with The Family Dog

And the World happily folds itself up

Like a map in love with its own territory

To join the Diggers as they circle the electric fire

Listening to their favorite stories

The rage of fair Achilles

And the struggles of a confidence man

Selling his most dangerous ideas

On a steamboat from St Louis to New Orleans

The Way She Laughs In the Bath

The way she laughs in the bath

The way she combs her long auburn hair

It doesn't matter if she misunderstands

The momentousness of it

Or inflates its scent

Until they can't breathe without making love

It doesn't matter what's going on out there

It's his duty and clear desire

To serve and protect her invading beauty

A poem for breakfast with the toast

One slipped under a saddle in Petaluma

A soft kiss on the back of her neck

Watching Peter Coyote do Hamlet in Bolinas

Short simple things

Burst and brought quickly to light

Then quietly lost in the complexities of the day

A White Sheet

Frank finds two hickory mashies in the Free Store

And gives Rikki and Sammy a call

As they idle at the curb

He flashes on a forgotten identity

He's still the registered owner of the Digger van

Passed from Dr Groom to Sammy

And now the most-wanted vehicle in California

This burst of adrenaline trips a well-hidden switch

And Frank's mind fills with darker insight

That comes too close to the Truth

Every moment of Love creates a world of Hate

In immediate defiance Frank decides to ask Erin tonight

And waves goodbye to his friends

The lovers wave back

Racing their bent and shotup shell

Up to Lincoln Park for a one-club match

Rejoicing in crystalline San Francisco

Chasing the sounds of old steel striking turf

And gutties spinning in limpid air

Until Sammy spots a white sheet

Coming up through the Golden Gate Bridge

The Be-In

On the foggydamp morning of the Human Be-In

Gary Snyder and Allen Ginsberg purify the ground

And establish a sacred perimeter by chanting a mix

Of traditional Hindu and Buddhist mantras

Parker takes closeups of Gary on the conch

And Allen gazing into the middle distance

Soon ten twenty thirty thousand hippies from everywhere

Are dropping their favorite acid and dancing in the wet grass

Quicksilver and The Dead stretching out guitar solos

Squinting at the fuzzy sun

Parker takes candids

Of hippies pale from the Fillmore underground

Meeting their bronze brothers from the suburbs

Gary

Allen

Michael

And Lenore reading their fifteen minutes of Love Poetry

Billy spraying black warning signs onstage

Freeway Ends

One Lane Ahead

Wake up

Tim Leary smiles aloof

Levitating two inches above recognition

Jerry Rubin and the Berkeley New Leftists

Denounce the Vietnam War through bad amplification

As the stoned dancers empty all Being

And fill their best Becoming

Parker takes a panorama shot

Of Frank and Erin's wedding

Her diamontine Dutch dress

Rising from a Florentine shell of golden auras

Dessy and Hardy stroll the crowd with walkie-talkies

Pretending to keep the Hells Angels in line

As Dessy spells out Cardoza for a Chronicle reporter

Her event's already a big success

When Owsley dressed as Uncle Sam

Parachutes down in the late afternoon

Followed by a lazy cloud

Of two thousand dollar bills

Jerry Garcia holds a Renaissance chord

And the comedown crowd finally responds

To Allen's karma call

By sunset the Polo Field is picked clean

The tribes have returned to their psychedelic bedrooms

The flatbed stage is back on Stanyan

And Dessy has found the way

Monterey Pop

The music festivals spread as the seasons turn

Everything political philosophical or poetic

Is eaten by rock and roll

From a handful of actors rebels and mystics

The Diggers are now a large organization

Coordinating media relations for the Haight

Everybody knows Dessy's story

How she started taking names at the crashpad

How she conceived the Human Be-In

Everybody knows how she pulled the Diggers together

After Peter Berg and Emmett Grogan disappeared

Everybody knows she invented the slogan

Today Is The First Day Of The Rest Of Your Life

And put the little girl on the poster beach

In the eyes of the media Dessy is the Diggers

So when she says its time for a Big Event

Something International

Monterey Pop instantly appears

LA sends The Mamas and The Papas Canned Heat

India sends Ravi Shankar

Chicago sends Otis Redding

London sends The Who Jimi Hendrix

The Haight sends Quicksilver Messenger Service

The Grateful Dead The Jefferson Airplane

Big Brother And The Holding Company

Chance finds Frank

Walking through the windsprung pines with Billy

Talking of present and ultimate concerns

The girls are sweet says Billy

But hippies can't write

Monterey Pop will be quickly forgotten

And rewritten by those who were never here

Hippies are too spontaneous

Too orgasmic

Too graphic for poetry

And the encoded commands of pure intelligence

If you're Weasel

I'm Crow

If you're Dionysus

I'm Apollo

I was you

I am you

And I'll always be you

I become more stable

More powerful

In your chaotic transformations

Of Mind and Material

Without my temporal continuity

Without the sure distance of my solar bow

The World would eclipse itself

In your frenzies of enthusiasm and probability

Today I see both vibrating horizons of time

And have decided to decide

No more writing stories in blood

No more acid politics

No more black magic kisses in the van

I'm going back to New York

Teach Wordsworth at City College

Take my dog on walks

And sharpen the tips of my poems

Well

Says Frank winking to the camera

I guess that leaves me to wander the World

In a minotaur mask

Carrying Monterey Pop

This fragile little apotheosis

This fierce all-too-human hope

In the hidden pockets of every tomorrow

Because you split first

Yes!

Every set takes it higher

Canned Heat fuzz the country blues

Otis shakes the stage with Motown moves

Ravi Shankar puts the audience in a Vedic trance

And Jimi comes twice burning his stratocaster

But Janis is the best

Stomp shouting out the cosmic blues

The wherever you are whatever you do cosmic blues

For three days two hundred thousand hippies

Jumpstart the Summer Of Love

Under the benign eye of the Monterey County Sheriff

Nobody's hassled or busted

The Beatles just came out with Sgt Pepper

The World is truly being born anew

They Don't Care

There's no two ways about it

Says Dr Groom fingering his earring

If you don't give up sex you'll die

You're four-ten four-eleven

And you weigh two-seventy

You need exercise and a healthy diet

With some willpower and these green pills

You can lose up to twenty pounds a month

You'll be able to walk unassisted again

You'll be able to drive a car

You'll have your own life back

I know your disciples are addicted to your services

Spiritual sex is their supreme fix

They don't want you to diet

They'll demand free sex every hour every day

Until you have a heart attack

Mankind is too greedy for Love

Too weak and resentful

Ask any other goddess

Take this moment and ask them now

Ask them in your mind

You already know their reply

Sure your people love and honor you

Like they love and honor a holy sow

They don't consider your sacrifice

Your physical and mental health

Look at yourself in the mirror

Where's the folksinger from West Virginia?

The girl who could play heavenly autoharp?

They've mistaken you for a whore in the Haight

No matter what you said

No matter what you gave

They took you for a whore and they don't care

They don't care if you bloat up

They don't care if you die

They only want to get off

And know when they can get off again

Your spiritual purity excites them

It runs well with their secret perversions

Dessy and I care Feather

Trust us

You must completely give up sex

Take these pills

And rejoin the Christian Church

God rejoices when a sinner repents

Of your thousands of lovers where is one man or woman

To stand by you now in your time of need?

I say the time of Free Love and Revolution is over

I say it's time to work and rejoin society

It's time to rededicate your soul to God

And His saving Grace

I forgive you

Dessy forgives you

Dionysus forgives you

Caesar forgives you

Prado the assassin forgives you

It'll be hard in the beginning

To feed and clothe yourself

To take those difficult first steps

But with faith in the Father your success is assured

It's not your Will but God's Will in you

That will bring your soul to Him

Your pagan libertine ways

Will melt like snow in the sacred flames

And He will reveal what works

He wants you to accomplish in His Name

I'll be honest with you

I was not always Christ

I was clever and vain

I wrote good books

But now I have perfect faith

And can truthfully say if you don't quit sex today

You'll die within a month

You must find the Courage to make the break

I think my years in medical school

Those nightmares as an intern

Sleeping on cots in the emergency ward

And the specialty papers I wrote for scientific journals

Have prepared me for the complexities of your case

You and I have seen many things with the Diggers Feather

But these experiences can't change the facts

Our reality is created and maintained by self-interest

I'll make you a partner in Groom Diet Enterprises

We'll multi-level market these algae pills

And buy a mansion on Nob Hill

You'll be the Groom Diet Girl

You'll be respected by high society

You'll be able to charge everything

Wear dresses and accessories from Saks

But it's not going to be easy

No one can promise you that

Survival is your highest spiritual duty

And salvation your daily goal

It'll take some time to rediscover your original sins

So Dessy has arranged for you to stay

At a luxury retreat in the Ben Hinnom Valley

Not far from Walnut Creek

With regular prayers and my pills

You'll be slim again

Reborn

No!

Ariadne!

Since we met on this island

I've become every human and divine identity

Waiting to say this

Theseus has gone

Man is overcome once again

He is the Eternal Recurrence

Ariadne I love you!

Letter To Miami

First tell Mom I'm safe I'm fine

I go to target practice daily

My story is well received

And now my mission is almost done

You've probably seen me on TV

Calling the kids of America to runaway

And come to the Haight for the Summer Of Love

I don't think any agent

Has been so far undercover so long

I know you'll be proud of me

I've willed the way to success

And I've willed myself back to you

You taught me to love America

You taught me to watch for Satanists

You taught me to watch for Communists

And Hate enabled me to find them

The FBI trafficking manual was useless

And Haight-Ashbury was a labyrinth

I knew LSD was the drug of choice

But the purest stuff was sold on the street

For no more than two or three dollars a hit

And usually the Diggers gave it away free

I knew the Sandoz link from Switzerland

Was under close surveillance

So checking out local sources

I discovered that Owsley was bankrolling everybody

Through sales of LSD from his mountain labs

And then everything made sense

The Haight is Hell

Behind the facade of flowers and Love

The Grateful Dead are Satan's Band

The Merry Pranksters are his Fools

The Hell's Angels are his Demons

And the Diggers are his Gravediggers

Making space in the black ancestral loam

For young hippies in love with pleasure

Who trade their immortal souls for passing delusions

So with logistical support from the CIA

And COINTELPRO backing from Hoover

I've rekindled the fiery pit

Created a new tophet in Gehenna

A new child sacrifice to God

During a final Digger event for TV

The Diggers will hand out free LSD

Calling it Owsley's masterpiece

When it's actually bad acid from our Army labs

Heavily cut with strychnine and speed

Hundred of hippies will die

Some will jump from burning windowsills

Some will drown in their burning vomit

The media will be tipped and tuned in

To broadcast my victory on the evening news

I am Dessy

I an Good

I am the Chosen One

Chosen by you and my Greater Father

To bring Peace to the World

From the Hate of Haight-Ashbury

Comes the Love of New America

From the chaotic Revolution comes the New World Order

Those who understand will give up their rights

Their children their conscience to survive

Those that resist will learn our efficiency

Yesterday I burned their precious Feather

And now the Diggers have no center

They fling themselves outward like mad comets

And inward like golden idols

The day the poison hits the street

Owsley's Reign Of Lies will end

And America will be purified by God's fiery breath

I've tried so hard to regain your Love Dad

What do you think of me now?

Am I a good cop?

Am I a good American?

Am I still a Cardoza?

Can I be your daughter again?

Can I come home?

Can I come home soon?

Death Of Hippie

The Diggers disintegrating

Some hanging with Black Panthers

Some split to New Mexico

Others back to greasepaint and spare change

Dessy rallies the core staff

For a Big Event mocking the media

For their hype of Haight-Ashbury

Time Magazine gives Hippie to the World

And now the Diggers take Hippie away

New Sense and common sense both say

Hippie's become profit and private property

It's time for Hippie to die

They nail redwood planks to the Frame Of Reference

Paint the yellow wood white

Hardy stretches out as Dessy's lamb

Smiling beatific

Nine new Diggers carry the weight

Frank and Erin

Rikki and Sammy

Dr Groom Parker and Toby out front

Joking with plum morning spectators

Handing out free hits of the deadly Dark Star

Dessy's icon of New America

Heraclitus barking directions

Down Haight to Market headed for the Financial District

TV trucks and reporters at every intersection

The buzzroar of news helicopters circling

Everyone too stoned or sleepless to anticipate the worst

Live anchors read Dessy's script

Today in San Francisco the Diggers

The revolutionary cell that brought us The Summer Of Love

Have organized Death Of Hippie

A protest march proclaiming The Fall of Haight-Ashbury

Over five hundred hippies are marching downtown

With The Last Hippie on a blasphemous horizontal cross

In a strong public show of solidarity

Local religious and political leaders

Have joined the Haight Independent Proprietors

In a statement denouncing the Diggers

As Red Terrorists

The Diggers were considered the masterminds

Of the hippie counterculture

The architects and social conscience of the Haight

Now that they're discredited and disbanding

The fear here in San Francisco is that the Summer Of Love

Will quickly decay into a long Winter Of Discontent

The camera zooms in on Hardy

Looking more like Jesus with each passing station

When the Diggers get him to Market Street

They find it lined on both sides with SWAT teams

Hunched behind Kevlar shields and heavy automatic weapons

When she sees the flashing headlights

Dessy says calmly I hate You

And fires at the chosen bulletproof vest

Rikki charges the line

Shouting Stop The Vietnam War!

Her head blown off by shotgun blasts

Sammy and Parker killed trying to save her

Dr Groom is Nietzsche insane

On his knees rocking and kissing her bloody torso

On his knees rocking and kissing her bloody torso

Contents

Page

1	Looking For The Perfect Rock
6	Flick The On Switch
11	Running From Reseda
16	The Vanity Of Man
25	Breakfast At Denny's
33	Buddha's Body
40	The One-Club Match
44	The Word After Beastly
47	A Small Jewel
49	The Guitar Man
53	Burrs
57	The Material Agent
64	First Tuesday
71	Crashpad
72	A Pipe Feeding Strawberry Creek
76	A Distinguished Guest
79	The Winning Streak
85	To Be Hip
88	The Day He Beat Bobby Fischer
96	Five-Mile Beach
104	The Elevators At Langley Porter

Page

112	In My Arms
119	Fruitvale
125	Dig The Diggers
132	The Curtains
135	Hexagrams
139	The Jack Of Spades
144	The Luckiest Day Of His Life
149	Poppies
150	Free Food
153	The Acid Test
158	Above The Center
169	The Trips Festival
170	Peter And Emmett Will Be Back Soon
175	Double Delight
177	Fillmore And Avalon
179	The Way She Laughs In The Bath
181	A White Sheet
183	The Be-In
186	Monterey Pop
192	They Don't Care
199	Letter To Miami
204	Death Of Hippie

The Author

Lawrence Johns is a philosopher and poet, the inventor of Field Language and founder of the city-state of Athenapolis. He is the author of a wide array of singular literary works, best known in Europe for *Sensazioni*, his empirical history of consciousness written in FL and published in Milan with an Italian preface and reading guide. Lawrence received his Ph.D. from The Graduate Theological Union in Berkeley and lives in Portland, Oregon where he directs The Walt Whitman School of Poetics and Conscious Publishing.

The Conscious Libraries

The Classic Library

1. Science And Myth, Gianfranco Spavieri

2. Love And Hate, Lawrence Johns

The Popular Library

1. The Golden Vortex, Nick Nelson

Conscious Publishing

POB 80262
Portland, Oregon 97280

www.consciouspublishing.com

*All Conscious Books,
including Special Editions,
can be ordered directly from our website.*

www.ingramcontent.com/pod-product-compliance
Lightning Source LLC
Chambersburg PA
CBHW031627160426
43196CB00006B/305